5 Days of Grace in The Father's Love

Women's Devotional

Maude E. McCullough

DEDICATION

To my Lord Jesus Christ, who is my dearest friend and confidant.

5 Days of Grace in The Father's Love

CONTENTS

Maude E. McCullough

ACKNOWLEDGMENTS

To my husband and partner for his love and patience. To my daughters for being my friendly helpers and encouragers. To my Pastors Jeffery and Misty Dorsey who continue to encourage the gift of God in my life. To Elder Marcella Jordan for her continued counsel and prayers.

DAY 1

Meditate on the scripture verses today and allow your soul to receive the love of the Father that is clearly demonstrated in His Word.

*For **God so loved** the world, that he gave his only begotten Son, that whosoever believeth in him should not perish, but have everlasting life.*

John 3:16 (KJV)

God 's love is clear. He demonstrated His love by the gift of His Son, Jesus. If you have accepted Jesus as payment for your sins and allow Him Lordship over your life, you are free to embrace this love in a relationship with God. You can also know Him as a loving Father and One who loves you deeply.

*But **God demonstrates His own love** for us in this: While we were still sinners Christ died for us..*

Romans 5:8 (NIV)

He loved us even when we were in sin. He displayed this love by sending Jesus to die for our sins on the cross to grant us access to His presence..

*But God, who is rich in mercy, for **his great love wherewith he loved us,***

*Even when we were dead in sins, hath quickened us together with Christ, (**by grace ye are saved;**)*

*And hath **raised us up together, and made us sit together in heavenly places in Christ Jesus:***

*That in the ages to come he might show the exceeding riches of his **grace** in his kindness toward us through Christ Jesus.*

*For **by grace are ye saved** through faith; and that not of yourselves: it is the gift of God:*

Ephesians 2:4-8 (KJV)

God's love is great towards us. He saved us by grace and positioned us in His beloved Son, Jesus. This is purely a gift from God because of His love for us.

*But I am like an olive tree flourishing in the house of God; **I trust in God's unfailing love** for ever and ever.*

Psalm 52:8 (NIV)

God's Love is unfailing!

Meditate on today's verses.

Write a reflection on what that verse means to you.

DAY 2

*Now our Lord Jesus Christ himself, and God, even our **Father, which hath loved us, and hath given us everlasting consolation and good hope** through grace, Comfort your hearts, and establish you in every good word and work.*

2Thessalonians 2:16 -17 (KJV)

His love has given us everlasting comfort and good hope. This hope will not disappoint us if we do not lose heart, but remain in His love.

In this was manifested the love of God toward us, *because that **God sent his only begotten Son into the world, that we might live through him.***

1 John 4:9 (KJV)

We can have an abundant life if we live through Jesus.

***This is love**: not that we loved God, **but he loved us** and **sent his Son** as an **atoning sacrifice** for our sins.*

1John 4:10 (NIV)

God's love was manifested for us in the act of Jesus coming into the world to die for our sins in order for us to have eternal life through Him.

The LORD hath appeared of old unto me, saying, Yea, I have loved thee with an **everlasting love***: therefore with lovingkindness have I drawn thee.*

Jeremiah 31:3 (KJV)

The Father's love is everlasting!

"Who **shall separate us from the love of Christ***? Shall trouble or hardship or persecution or famine or nakedness or danger or sword? As it is written: "For your sake we face death all day long; we are considered as sheep to be slaughtered." No, in all these things we are more than conquerors through him who loved us.* **For I am convinced that neither death nor life, neither angels nor demons, neither the present nor the future, nor any powers, neither height nor depth, nor anything else in all creation, will be able to separate us from the love of God that is in Christ Jesus our Lord."**

Romans 8:35-39 (NIV)

Nothing can ever separate us from the love of God in Christ Jesus.

Meditate on today's verses.

Write a reflection on what that verse means to you.

Maude E. McCullough

DAY 3

I led them with cords of **human kindness,** *with* **ties of love.** *To them I was like one who* **lifts a little child to the cheek and bent down to feed them.**

Hosea 11:4 (NIV)

God drew us to Him with love. He cares for us as little children, and nurtures us with in His Word.

But when the kindness and love of God our Savior appeared, *he saved us, not because of righteous things we had done, but because of his mercy. He saved us through the washing of rebirth and renewal by the Holy Spirit.*

Titus 3:4-5 (NIV)

The Father's love comes with kindness and a great deal of action. His love is agape love. A love that has nothing to do with our deserving of it, but because of His goodwill.

And we have known and believed **the love that God hath to us.** **God is love;** *and he that dwelleth in love dwelleth in God, and God in him.*
1John 4:16 (KJV)

The Father is love. Receive that love as you live in Him.

*"As the Father has loved me, **so have I loved you**. **Abide in my love**. If you keep my commandments, you will **abide in my love**, just as I have kept my Father's commandments and abide in his love. These things I have spoken to you, that **my joy may be in you**, and that your **joy may be full.** "This is my commandment, that you love one another as I have loved you. Greater love has no one than this, that someone lay down his life for his friends. You are my friends if you do* what I *command you. No longer do I call you servants, for the servant does not know what his master is doing; but I **have called you friends**, for all that I have heard from my Father I have made known to you. **You did not choose me, but I chose you** and appointed you..."*

John 15:9-16a (ESV)

We can abide in God's love through Jesus. He chose us. He laid down His life for us. Our joy can be complete if we live in Jesus and obey Him.

Meditate on today's verses.

Write a reflection on what that verse means to you.

DAY 4

*But thou, O LORD, art a **shield for me; my glory, and the lifter up of mine head.***
Psalm 3:3(KJV)

God's love is a shield of protection for us from the enemy and He lifts our head and times of depression and in despair.

*What is man, that thou art **mindful of him**? and the **son of man, that thou visitest him**?*
Psalm 8:4 (KJV)

God as a father is mindful of us. He cares about what concerns us. He visits us with His divine presence.

*For thou hast made him a little lower than the angels, and **hast crowned him with glory and honour.***
Psalm 8:5 (KJV)

As His children, God has crowned us with glory and honor to be displayed on the Earth.

*"So God created man in **his own image,** in the image of God created he him; **male and female created he them.**"*

Genesis 1:27 (KJV)

God loved you so, that He created you in His own image!

Christ loved us and gave himself up for us *as a fragrant offering and sacrifice to God.*

Ephesians 5:2 (KJV)

Jesus gave Himself up willing for us because He loves us.

There is no fear in love; ***but perfect love casteth out fear:*** *because fear hath torment. He that feareth is not made perfect in love.*

1John 4:18 (KJV)

God's love is intended to cast out fear. In Him fear has no right to torment you. Let His love get perfected in you in order for you to be freed from fear. Learn of Him, come to know His ways, follow and obey His Word.

<u>Meditate on today's verses.</u>

Write a reflection on what that verse means to you.

DAY 5

Your love, O LORD, reaches to the heavens,
your faithfulness to the skies.

Your righteousness is like the mighty mountains,
your justice like the great deep.
O LORD, you preserve both man and beast.

How priceless is your unfailing love!
Both high and low among men
find refuge in the shadow of your wings."

Psalm 36:5 -7 (NIV)

God's love is priceless and it will never fail. Man's love can fail and be conditional, but God's love will never run out.

I will praise the Lord, who counsels me; even at night my heart instructs me.
Psalm 16:7 (NIV)

Our great and awesome Father gives us counsel and instruction. We are His sheep and He is our Shepherd, whose voice He promises we will hear if we remain in Him.

*Thou wilt show me the path of life: in thy **presence is fulness of joy; at thy right hand there are pleasures for evermore.***
Psalm 16:11 (KJV)

Joy awaits us every time we come into His presence!

*And it shall come to pass in that day, that his **burden shall be taken away from off thy shoulder, and his yoke from off thy neck, and the yoke shall be destroyed because of the anointing.***
Isaiah 10:27 (KJV)

He removes our burdens and destroys the yoke of the enemy off our necks.

*Let your conversation be without covetousness; and be content with such things as ye have**: for he hath said, I will never leave thee, nor forsake thee.***
Hebrews 13:5 (KJV)

God our Father promises to never leave us nor forsake us. What can man do to us with Him on our side?!

Meditate on today's verses.

Write a reflection on what that verse means to you.

Maude E. McCullough

Now take the next five (5) days set some time aside to read the daily Scripture verses. As you read each day, pray for God to speak to you through the verses. Meditate on what God is speaking to you in the in His Word. Open your heart and let Him meet you in His Word. Pay special attention to the ways He describes His love to you. Then write your reflection on what these verses mean to you.

Open my eyes, that I may behold wondrous things out of Your law.
Psalm 119:18 (KJV)

Maude E. McCullough

DAY 1

"Can a mother forget her nursing child? Can she feel no love for the child she has borne? But even if that were possible, I would not forget you! See, I have written your name on the palms of my hands."

Isaiah 49:15-16 (NLT)

Within your temple, O God, we meditate on your unfailing love.

Psalm 48:9 (NIV)

But you, O Lord, are a compassionate and gracious God, slow to anger, abounding in love and faithfulness.

Psalm 86:15 (NIV)

"For I know the plans I have for you," declares the LORD, "plans to prosper you and not to harm you, plans to give you hope and a future."

Jeremiah 29:11 (NIV)

<u>Meditate on today's verses.</u>

Write a reflection on what that verse means to you.

DAY 2

The LORD your God in your midst, The Mighty One, will save; He will rejoice over you with gladness, He will quiet you with His love, He will rejoice over you with singing."

Zephaniah 3:17 (NKJV)

As the Father has loved me, so have I loved you. Now remain in my love.

John 15:9 (NIV)

"Within your temple, O God, we meditate on your unfailing love."

Psalm 48:9 (NIV)

Because of the LORD's great love we are not consumed, for his compassions never fail. They are new every morning; great is your faithfulness. I say to myself, "The LORD is my portion; therefore I will wait for him." The LORD is good to those whose hope is in him, to the one who seeks him. "

Lamentations 3:22 – 25 (NIV)

<u>Meditate on today's verses.</u>

Write a reflection on what that verse means to you.

DAY 3

"For you created my inmost being; you knit me together in my mother's womb. I praise you because I am fearfully and wonderfully made; your works are wonderful, I know that full well. How precious to me are your thoughts, O God!

How vast is the sum of them! Were I to count them, they would outnumber the grains of sand."

Psalm 139:13 -14, 17- 18 (NIV)

"The word of the LORD came to me, saying, "Before I formed you in the womb I knew you, before you were born I set you apart."....

Jeremiah 1:4-5 (NIV)

"For I the LORD thy God will hold thy right hand, saying unto thee, Fear not; I will help thee."

Isaiah 41:13 (KJV)

<u>Meditate on today's verses.</u>

Write a reflection on what that verse means to you.

DAY 4

"Are not five sparrows sold for two farthings, and not one of them is forgotten before God? But even the very hairs of your head are all numbered. Fear not therefore: ye are of more value than many sparrows."

Luke 12:6-7 (KJV)

"Give thanks to the God of heaven. His love endures forever."

Psalm 136:26 (NIV)

"See what great love the Father has lavished on us, that we should be called children of God! And that is what we are! The reason the world does not know us is that it did not know him."

1 John 3:1 (NIV)

And hope maketh not ashamed; because the love of God is shed abroad in our hearts by the Holy Ghost which is given unto us.

Romans 5:5 (KJV)

Meditate on today's verses.

Write a reflection on what that verse means to you.

DAY 5

"I trust in God's unfailing love forever and ever."
Psalm 52:8b (NIV)

That he would grant you, according to the riches of his glory, to be strengthened with might by his Spirit in the inner man; That Christ may dwell in your hearts by faith; that ye, being rooted and grounded in love, May be able to comprehend with all saints what is the breadth, and length, and depth, and height; And to know the love of Christ, which passeth knowledge, that ye might be filled with all the fulness of God.

Ephesians3:16-19 (KJV)

He brought me to the banqueting house, and his banner over me was love [for love waved as a protecting and comforting banner over my head when I was near him].

Song of Solomon 2:4 (AMP)

Meditate on today's verses.

Write a reflection on what that verse means to you.

What must I do to be saved?

This is the most important question one can ask.

Many believe there are many ways to salvation. Many believe that being a good person will get them to heaven. According to the Bible this is not true.

> **James 2:10** says: *"For whoever keeps the whole law (good deeds) and yet stumbles in one point, he has become guilty of all."*

The Bible makes it very clear that all are sinners. No matter how good you, and those around you, think you are, you are a sinner.

- Believing in a god will not save you.
- Church membership and doing religious activities will not save you.
- Giving money to the church or to the poor will not save you.
- Volunteering your time to charitable activities will not save you.
- Living a moral life will not save you.
- Changing your behavior will not save you.
- Observing certain days or other rules and regulations will not save you or keep you saved.

It takes blood to pay for sin, for Scripture says:

In fact, the law requires that nearly everything be cleansed with blood, and without the shedding of blood there is no forgiveness.

Hebrews 9:22 (NIV)

For all have sinned, and fall short of the glory of God;

Romans 3:23 (NKJV)

For the wages of sin is death; but the gift of God is eternal life through Jesus Christ our Lord.

Romans 6:23 (KJV)

"And the testimony is this, that God has given us eternal life, and this life is in His Son. He who has the Son has the life; he who does not have the Son of God does not have the life. These things I have written to you who believe in the name of the Son of God, that you may know that you have eternal life, and that you may continue to believe in the name of the Son of God"

1 John 5:11-13 (NKJV)

For God so loved the world, that he gave his only begotten Son, that whosoever believeth in him should not perish, but have everlasting life. For God sent not his Son into the world to condemn the world; but that the world through him might be saved.

John 3:16-17 (KJV)

But God demonstrated his own love toward us, in that, while we were still sinners, Christ died for us.

Romans 5:8 (NKJV)

That if confess with your mouth the Lord Jesus, and believe in your heart that God has raised him from the dead, you will be saved. For with the heart one believes unto righteousness; and with the mouth confession is made unto salvation.

Romans 10:9-10 (NKJV)

For whosoever shall call upon the name of the Lord shall be saved.

Romans 10:13 (KJV)

For by grace are you have been saved through faith; and that not of yourselves: it is the gift of God: Not of works, lest anyone should boast.

Ephesians 2:8-9 (NKJV)

The Bible tells us that "God . . . commandeth all men everywhere to repent" (Acts 17:30). This repentance is a change of mind that agrees with God that one is a sinner, and also agrees with what Jesus did for us on the cross.

47

Salvation is a gift from God that only requires our belief, confession and acceptance. When we receive salvation from God, it's much more than a ticket to heaven. Salvation includes eternal rescue from sin and its consequences. It also means healing, preservation, and deliverance. When we get saved we allow God to bring His healing, deliverance and preservation into our lives. Salvation also includes access to an abiding relationship with God the Father and His Son Jesus Christ.

Salvation is a deliberate decision to receive Jesus into our hearts as Lord and Savior. If you would like to receive Jesus Christ as your Lord and Savior, you can do it right now! Pray this prayer:

> **"Jesus, I accept You as my Lord and Savior. I confess that You are the Son of God and that You died for my sins on the cross. I ask for forgiveness of my sins. I believe in my heart that You were raised from the dead and in You I can live an abundant life. Thank you Heavenly Father for saving me in the Jesus name I pray, Amen."**

If you prayed this prayer you are Saved! Welcome to the family of God! The angels are rejoicing!

<u>Continuing in your Christian Growth</u>:

God's Word tell us *not to forsake "the assembling of ourselves together." (Hebrews 10:25)*

Your relationship with God is best grown in an environment with other believers that desire to walk in relationship with Christ as well. So commit to a Bible believing church where the Word of God is taught, and a personal relationship with Jesus Christ is encouraged. Doing this will give you support and accountability in your walk with God. It will also be a place that will help you walk in your purpose in God.

Also as a new child of God you can share the same assurance in God's Word that tells us:

"being confident of this very thing, that He who has begun a good work in you will complete it until the day of Christ Jesus."

Philippians 1:6 (NKJV)

Therefore if any man be in Christ, he is a new creature: old things are passed away; behold, all things are become new.
2 Corinthians 5:17 (NKJV)
Abide in me, and I in you. As the branch cannot bear fruit of itself, except it abide in the vine; no more can ye, except ye abide in me.

I am the vine, ye are the branches: He that abideth in me, and I in him, the same bringeth forth much fruit: for without me ye can do nothing.

John 15:4(KJV)

Then said Jesus to those Jews which believed on him, If ye continue in my word, then are ye my disciples indeed; And ye shall know the truth, and the truth shall make you free.

John 8:31-32(KJV)

If the Son therefore shall make you free, ye shall be free indeed.

John 8:36 (NKJV)

Scripture referenced is taken from the New International Version Bible (NIV), The King James Version bible (KJV), New King James Version bible (NKJV), New Living Translation bible(NLT), and English Standard Version (ESV).

All emphasis added to Scripture are added by the author.

Maude E. McCullough

BIBLIOGRAPHY

New King Version James Bible copyright 1982 by Thomas Nelson, Inc.

New Living Translation (NLT) copyright Holy Bible 1966, 2004, 2007, by Tyndale House Foundation

English Standard Version (ESV) copyright 2001 by Crossway Bibles. A division of Good News Publishers.

Amplified Bible (AMP) copyright 1954, 1958, 1962, 1964, 1965, 1987 by the Lockman Foundation.

Maude E. McCullough

ABOUT THE AUTHOR

Maude McCullough is a minister of the Gospel who has a passion to see people walk in an intimate relationship with God. She is a Pastor and holds a Masters Degree in Faith Based Counseling. She is a wife and mother of four children and grandmother of one.

Other Books from

The Father's Embrace Devotionals for Living

14 Day Devotions in the Names of God

14 Day Devotions in the Book of Psalms

14 Day Devotions in the Book of Ephesians

5 Days of Grace in the Father's Love

Men's Devotional

5 Days of Grace in the Father's Love

Youth Devotional

The Old Man and The New Man

The Renewed Mind

Made in the USA
Charleston, SC
11 May 2012